TEACHINGS OF MOHAMMAD

OTHER TITLES IN THIS SERIES

TEACHINGS OF HINDUISM

TEACHINGS OF BUDDHA

TEACHINGS OF JESUS CHRIST

THE HADEES-SHREEF TEACHINGS OF MOHAMMAD

Ajanta Chakravarty

RIDER

LONDON · SYDNEY · AUCKLAND · JOHANNESBURG

1 3 5 7 9 10 8 6 4 2

Copyright © Ajanta Chakravarty 1997

Ajanta Chakravarty has asserted her moral right to be identified as the author of this work in accordance with the Copyright, Design and Patents Act 1988.

All rights reserved. No part of this publication may be reproduced, stored in a retrieval system, or transmitted in any form or by any means, electronic, mechanical, photocopying or otherwise, without the prior permission of the copyright owner.

First published in 1997 by Shishti Publishers, India.
This edition published in 1998 by Rider, an imprint of
Ebury Press
Random House UK Ltd
Random House
20 Vauxhall Bridge Road
London SW1V 2SA

Random House Australia (Pty) Ltd
20 Alfred Street
Milsons Point, Sydney
New South Wales, 2016 Australia

Random House New Zealand Limited
18 Poland Road, Glenfield
Auckland 10, New Zealand

Random House South Africa (Pty) Limited
Endulini, 5A Jubilee Road
Parktown 2193, South Africa

Random House UK Limited Reg. No. 954009

Papers used by Rider Books are natural, recyclable products made from wood grown in sustainable forests.

Printed and bound in Great Britain by CPD, Wales

A CIP catalogue record for this book is available from the British Library

ISBN 0-7126-7187-0

*In memory of Smt Maya Majumdar
— whose dreamchild this was!*

Preface

The origin of life on earth is a contentious issue between scientists and believers. Scientists search for the truth, trying to prove its existence through rigorous experimentation, leaving no room for ambiguities. Believers, on the other hand take the existence of the Supreme Truth as granted; the rest follows thereafter with irrefutable logic.

What is generally overlooked is that between these conflicting views, there is a definite common factor about the beginning of life, the coming into existence of living matter. This is the manifestation of the 'life-force' or what has been described by many as the 'vital elan'. This force must have a 'life space' around it to provide for its sustenance and reproduction. The two must fit precisely and harmoniously for life to grow, flourish and evolve into its many different forms.

There were calamities too. The iceage, the submergences, earthquakes, tornadoes, avalanches, and the volcanic eruptions changed life space so dramatically that entire species were wiped out. There were other disasters, less dramatic but of no less magnitude. Exhaustion of natural food resources, spoiling of natural habitat, and overcrowding of life space led to large-scale disasters. The changes in environment meant that the vital elan had two options, either to adapt to the changes or be annihilated. Very often it was the latter because the species lacked the ability to adjust to the oncoming changes and reorient themselves until it was too late.

When man finally appeared on earth, he was as exposed to all the vagaries of life space as other species. But he was intelligent. He could observe, reason, deduce and apply the core of his thinking to harness the life space rather than be driven by it. He searched actively for means of enhancing the 'vital elan' and his quest was both in the physical world outside and the spiritual world within himself. The last gave rise to religion.

It is often thought that primordial man was a not-so-clever animal, who blindly worshipped the forces of nature – the rocks, trees, streams, clouds and the stars. Many have expressed doubts about organized religion on account of its being an atavistic throwback to the dark ages of the past. In today's world of fast-paced determinism, religion is often publicly scorned but privately engaged in to propitiate the very same forces that may in some way make life space more acceptable to us. And in this cauldron of conflicting desires and ambitions, the true significance of religion and the religious teachings and precepts get lost.

Man's search for tools with which to master his environment led to science. But prior to that, he had evolved language, without which no development would have been possible. Language gave him the means to communicate his thoughts, his feelings, his enquiries with others. His superior brain enabled the processing of loose, unstructured information into systematic forms. This was knowledge, the most powerful tool at his command. He could use it for harmony, growth and peace or for wanton annihilation. What he needed were guidelines for implementing his knowledge. He sought the power of wisdom. And once again, he turned, both to the forces outside to understand the mysteries of nature and within, to know the truth of his very being. He wanted to learn from the Masters who had drunk deep of the springs of wisdom and on whose teachings were founded the great religions, the pathways of discernment.

It must be noted that many religions have come into being and almost as many have disappeared without trace. They could not measure up to the changing demands of life space. Those which survived went through many trials and tribulations, each tempering its core values for greater robustness. Their Masters, often coming at the darkest hour, brought messages of hope. Of good sense. Of homespun, sensible practices which could be adopted by all, irrespective of birth and position. Unfortunately, the passage of time invariably obscured these precepts. The primary cause for this was that the language forms underwent spatial and temporal changes, restructuring and reinterpreting. These variations proceeded to filter into common usage according to their ability of easing Man's understanding. Over time, the regular languages changed their forms so radically that the scriptural languages were rendered impotent. Thus the wisdom inherent in them was lost to new generations.

This series of books attempts to rediscover and reinterpret some of the teachings from the scriptures of a few mainstream religions, in a form suitable for absorption by the twentieth century person poised on the threshold of the twenty-first. The kind of world we will make then will depend to a great extent on the wisdom that precedes every small or big decision. Perhaps the information in this book will help in reinforcing the learning for making a better and more beautiful life space for humanity at large.

TEACHINGS OF MOHAMMAD

If the history of the world were to be stitched into one great tapestry, distinctly similar patterns would be seen from one end to another as messiahs arose, preached the message of truth, love and goodness and others followed them as the chosen ones.

Of the great religious leaders of the world, Mohammad is probably closer to us in time than any other. As he stood on a mountain top one day, his senses were dazzled by the vision of an immense figure standing astride the world, with his head far, far above and beyond the clouds. Mohammad shut his eyes but when he opened them again, the vision was still there.

Then he heard the vision speak: "O Mohammad! You are the messenger of God and I am Gabriel."

What Mohammad heard that day has come down to us

as the Holy Quran. Many of the Quranic utterances are philosophic in content, which the ordinary man may not have been able to relate to his daily activities. For this purpose, the Prophet (as Mohammad came to be known as) enunciated the "Hadees Shareef" which contain his down-to-earth, simple yet deeply moving homilies to guide an average man in leading a good life.

This volume is an attempt to interpret some of these teachings in a crisp, sharp focus for easy perusal by today's busy readers. The resemblance between many of these precepts and those of the Upanishads of the Bible are striking enough to make us pause and wonder at the eternity of the values that have sustained human life through the ages.

Honour your guest as you would your God.

Keep your heart free from the stains of avarice.

A good man is bound to his honour like a horse to a post.

Share your food. Eat together. Feel content.

A guest leaving should be escorted with due courtesy to the front door.

A guest should not outstay his welcome.

Those who ill-treat others do not win Allah's favour.

True repentance wins Allah's forgiveness.

Resolve dissensions through discussions.

Forbear from ill-treating others. It throws your own mind into turmoil.

Beware of the tears of the oppressed; they sparkle in the sky like fire flies.

Beware of the pleadings of the oppressed; they pray to Allah for justice and Allah is all just.

The cries of the persecuted rise up to Allah. Nothing can stop them.

Poor is the man whose life shows no good deed.

Those who usurp the wealth of orphans burn in the fires of hell.

The man who ploughs waste land and plants crops on it establishes his ownership of the land.

Waste not. Store food grains for the year of drought.

Kill the snake which enters your house.

Curse not the cock that crows at dawn; it merely calls you to prayer.

A repentant sinner is as good as a pious man.

Exchange the wages of sin with true penitence.

He sins doubly who blames others for his misdeeds.

Give everyone his due.

Satan is the ungrateful friend of every spendthrift.

Dine well. Sup well. But waste not.

One who curses others cannot live with one who speaks the truth.

Do not be vain or proud.

Let the birds stay peacefully in their nests.

Do not shun your relatives.

The results of severing relations with your own can be felt in this life.

A trustee should protect wealth unceasingly and return it to the rightful owner.

He who serves the wretched lives in the garden of Heaven.

The unbeliever regresses from the truth.

Man dies before his hopes do.

The aging man craves longevity.

Eat what you can digest.

Wash your hands before and after eating.

This life is but a pleasant illusion.

If you cannot share your table with your servant, at least share a part of your food with him for he laboured in heat and smoke to cook it.

A man with wealth to bestow should not delay in making his will.

A murderer cannot be the beneficiary of his victim's will.

That man has achieved excellence who does good unto others.

That man errs who reads the Quran but does not obey its teachings.

Motive is more important than the deed.

Giving to the destitute does not deplete wealth.

Earn your living by righteous means.

Happy is the man who is content with what he has.

Beware of debt. At night, it brings, worry and during the day, insult.

A debt-ridden man breaks promises and tells many lies.

Never befoul three places: water source, thoroughfare, shade.

Set a standard for weights and measures.

Do not cheat in weighing.

Sinners are they who take in full measure but give in smaller measure.

That is no feast where only the rich are invited and not the poor.

A sinner is he who has different words in his heart and on his tongue.

A miser deprives himself first (of the pleasure of giving).

Refrain from anger.

Refrain from unnecessary arguments.

As medicine sours honey, so does anger besmirch honour.

If you feel angry, sit down quietly; if possible, lie down quietly.

True heroism lies in the conquest of anger.

Never judge anything while angry.

Reconsider before acting.

There is no worship superior to clean thoughts.

Plant trees. Sow seeds in fertile fields. These are the acts of true philanthropy.

Learn and teach. Teach and learn.

Satan fears an honest man more than a hundred worshippers.

Knowledge is the road to destination heaven.

He who seeks knowledge seeks Allah.

Knowledge is in the treasure-chest and questions are the keys.

A teacher should not be so strict that the pupils run away in fear.

Ignorance is the greatest of all poverty.

Studying for one hour every night is better than praying all night.

The learned man who instructs others but does not follow his own advice is like the lamp which gives light to others but burns its own wick.

Intelligence is the leader of men.

A man is known by his intelligence.

A man without kindness is poor indeed.

The generous man is like a grain of rice from which grow many more grains.

A man who takes back a gift is like a dog eating his own vomit.

Every good deed is equal to an act of generosity.

Difficult times are the precursor of patience.

Happiness does not lie in wealth but in the hearts of men.

Wretched are the slaves to wealth.

As the head is to the body, so patience to honour.

Silence is the ornament of the learned and the clock of the ignorant.

Most troubles arise from words.

Restraining your anger is one of the best ways of worship.

Match the task to the capability.

Malice is surely worse than misdemeanour.

Piety will go as your companion to the afterworld.

Help your neighbours.

That man sins who feasts without helping a hungry neighbour.

If you must take a vow, keep it.

Marriage is the strongest foundation of friendship.

Do not be afraid of men.

Food for two can be shared by three.

Honour and hatred cannot coexist.

Do not sell the fruit till it is ripe.

Intoxication leads to greater evils.

Pay the labourer before his perspiration dries.

Teachings of Mohammad

Man lusts for forbidden fruit.